THIS BOOK BELONGS TO:

MY CAT RECORD BOOK

RACHAEL HALE

Bulfinch Press
New York • Boston

CONTENTS

COLLAR

IDENTITY TAG

FOOD BOWL

WATER BOWL

TOYS

SUITABLE KITTEN FOOD

LITTER BOX

PLACE PHOTO
HERE

I was born on

There were kittens in my litter

Date I came home

Address of family home

CHOOSING MY NAME

Names that were considered

Inspiration for my name

MY BREED

I am a

We are known for

BEST FEATURES

My eyes are

My paws are

My ears are

My whiskers are

GRANDFATHER

Birthplace

Date

FATHER

Birthplace

Date

FAMILY TREE

GRANDMOTHER

Birthplace

Date

MOTHER

Birthplace

Date

PLACE PHOTO
HERE

MY FAMILY

My owner is

We live at

Family members

Other pets

Other relatives

Neighbors

GROWING UP

SPECIAL MOMENTS

BIRTHDAYS

Year

Gifts

Party guests

Year

Gifts

Party guests

Year

Gifts

Party guests

Year

Gifts

Party guests

PLACE PHOTO
HERE

BIRTHDAYS

Year

Gifts

Party guests

Year

Gifts

Party guests

Year

Gifts

Party guests

Year

Gifts

Party guests

MY FAVORITE TOYS

OUTINGS

BEST FRIENDS

MY FAVORITE PASTIMES

PLACE PHOTO
HERE

MY FAVORITE PASTIMES

MY FAVORITE PLACES TO SLEEP

VACATIONS

ADVENTURES

ACHIEVEMENTS

ANNOYING HABITS

PLACE PHOTO HERE

GROOMING

PLACE PHOTO
HERE

PAW PRINTS

TRAINING

Age/Length/Weight

Date	Age	Length	Weight

VISITS TO THE VET

Date	Illness	Treatment

WORMING

Date _____ Date _____ Date _____ Date _____

VACCINATION

Date	Vaccine	Date	Vaccine

IMPORTANT ADDRESSES

Name

Address

Phone

Name

Address

Phone

Name

Address

Phone

Name

Address

Phone

Michael Clarke

Bulfinch Press

Time Warner Book Group
1271 Avenue of the Americas, New York, NY 10020
Visit our Web site at www.bulfinchpress.com

First North American Edition

Published by arrangement with PQ Publishers Limited

ISBN 0-8212-5697-1
Library of Congress Control Number 2004113256

Designed by Kylie Nicholls

PRINTED IN CHINA

CHAT

KITTEN

CAT

KATZE

KAT

CHATON

KATJE